AF573987

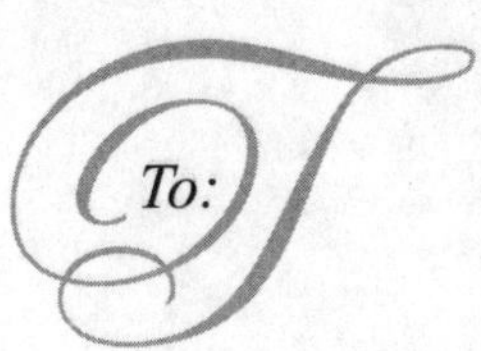
To:

From:

Date:

INTERNATIONAL

BIBLICAL FOUNDATIONS FOR A NEW BELIEVER

Biblical Foundations for a New Believer

Guillermo Maldonado

Our Vision

The objective of our mission is to spiritually feed God's people through preaching, teaching and the written word, and to take the Word of God everywhere it is needed.

Biblical Foundations for a New Believer

ISBN: 1-59272-089-7

First Edition 2005

Cover designed by:
GM International - Design Department

Interior Design by:
Luis Bravo - GM International

Category:
Biblical Foundations for a New Believer

Published by:
GM International
13651 SW 143 Ct. #101, Miami, FL 33186
(305) 233-3325 Fax (305) 675-5770

Printed by:
GM International
Printed in Colombia

Dedication

Throughout the years, God has stirred my heart with great passion for the lost souls; the lives for which Jesus gave up His own life on the cross. People with whom our heavenly Father wants to spend eternity with. Many people hear the message of salvation and accept it, but later, because of lack of knowledge, they are unable to grow and attain God's promises, receive the fullness of His joy and the power that He wants for us to have. I dedicate this book to these believers, may you find the answers to every question that rises up during your early walk with Christ. I pray for God to anoint every word written in this book so they can fulfill their purpose in you.

Acknowledgements

First, I want to thank the author and redeemer of my life; to Him who gave up His life to save mine. Jesus, thank you for your mercy and grace upon my life. Separate from you, I can do nothing. I also want to thank everyone who has embraced the vision and who work, day by day, together with me to guide the new believer in his path.

Index

Introduction

Throughout my years in the ministry, I have had the opportunity to know a great number of people who after receiving Jesus as Lord, have no idea where to go, what to do, or what steps to take in the Lord's path. This is what led me, with the help of the Holy Spirit, to write this book. Its purpose is to guide the new believer in his first steps as a new Christian. I, too, was a new believer once, and like many of you, I had many questions, including, "What is salvation?" "Where do I begin?" "What does God expect from me?" "What are my responsibilities?" "What am I allowed to do, and what am I not supposed to do?" These, and many more questions, come up during the early stages of our Christian walk.

Sadly, some believers never mature spiritually. One reason for this is that they never received the proper Biblical foundation. If the foundation is not firm, the rest of the "building" will be weak and fall with the slightest burst of wind.

It is my constant prayer that not one single soul be lost because of lack of direction or knowledge. This is the reason I decided to write this manual. I pray that it will be a great blessing to you, that you will be strengthened in your Christian walk and that your life be one of victory.

Guillermo Maldonado
Pastor

1

Eternal Salvation

Many concepts, religions and traditions guide humanity. But, regardless of these, there still remains emptiness in every human being, which he tries to fill with what seems appropriate at the moment. He tries to satisfy himself with fame, alcohol, drugs, sex, work, money, religion, and much more. He exhausts every avenue, but in the end, finds it impossible to fill the emptiness in his heart. God is the only one who can make us feel whole through a close relationship with Him.

"[11]...has made everything beautiful in its time. Also He has put eternity in their hearts...". Ecclesiastes 3.11

The little bit of eternity that the Lord has placed in humanity can only be filled by something eternal. This is the reason why worldly and material things can't fill this emptiness. Many people think that believing in God automatically guarantees their salvation and that they are God's children on their way to heaven. But, the Word of God doesn't teach this. Scripture teaches that we are His creation, but we are not all God's children.

Once you understand that man has emptiness in his heart, that he is a sinner by nature, and that it is necessary to be a child of God, the following questions should be answered: How can I go to heaven? How can I fill this emptiness? How do I find the truth? If you have been asking yourself these questions, then, with God's help, I will answer them based on God's Word. The first thing you must know is:

1. Salvation is free

"For the wages of sin is death, but the gift of God is eternal life in Christ Jesus our Lord." Romans 6.23

Going to heaven is free; there is nothing you can do to earn your salvation. Many people try to gain access into heaven through their good works, but it is only through the death and resurrection of our Lord Jesus Christ that we are saved, and this, by the grace of God.

"[8]For by grace you have been saved through faith, and that not of yourselves; it is the gift of God." Ephesians 2.8

2. All men are sinners

"[23]for all have sinned and fall short of the glory of God." Romans 3.23

Too many people boast about being good. They claim that they never hurt anybody and think that being good guarantees their passage into heaven. The Word of God teaches that from the moment that Adam sinned, every person that cames after him is born in sin, and because every person is a sinner, he can't save himself. Everybody, at one time or another, has lied, stolen, coveted or committed adultery; we have all sinned.

God is good and merciful. He doesn't want to punish humanity. He loves the world, but because of our sin, He must discipline us. God loves every sinner, but hates sin. It is because of this that God faced the dilemma of how to deal with us and His answer came through His Son Jesus who came into this world to lay down his life, to be crucified, to die and to rise up again. His sacrifice changes our lives; it cleanses us from our sin and restores our relationship with God.

"16For God so loved the world that He gave His only begotten Son, that whoever believes in Him should not perish but have everlasting life." John 3.16

3. Knowing Jesus as the Son of God

Who is Jesus?

a. **Jesus is the Son of God. He is one hundred percent God and one hundred percent man.**

"[1]In the beginning was the Word, and the Word was with God, and the Word was God. [14]And the Word became flesh and dwelt among us, and we beheld His glory, the glory as of the only begotten of the Father, full of grace and truth." John 1.1, 14

b. **Jesus is the only mediator between God and men.**

"[5]For there is one God and one Mediator between God and men, the Man Christ Jesus."
1 Timothy 2.5

Why is Jesus the only mediator between God and men?

Jesus is the only being that is God and man at the same time; therefore, He understands God and man. He knows the heart of the Father and His righteousness, as much as He understands the heart of man and sin. Jesus is the only one who can reconcile God and man. Worldly religions honor men as if they were gods, but none of them has the true God. Christianity is different than any worldly religion because Jesus is God and man at the same time.

"[20]...and by Him to reconcile all things to Himself, by Him, whether things on earth or things in heaven, having made peace through the blood of His cross." Colossians 1.20

c. Jesus is the way.

The only way to go to the Father; the only way to go into heaven; the only way to receive salvation; and the only way our sin can be forgiven is to recognize, accept and invite Jesus to be our personal Lord and Savior.

"[6]Jesus said to him, "I am the way, the truth, and the life. No one comes to the Father except through Me." John 14.6

What did Jesus do for you?

He died for your sin.

Jesus was crucified. He was resurrected on the third day and is now sitting at the right hand of the Father. Through His death, He paid for your sin, rebellion, sickness and iniquity. Through His sacrifice, you received, by grace, every blessing He has in store for you, along with salvation. He paid the price for your reconciliation at the cross.

How do you receive the gift of salvation?

You receive salvation by faith. Some people have a distorted way of understanding faith. They think that mental agreement is the same as believing God; this is far from the truth because we must believe wholeheartedly, not just with our mind. Some people only search for God, and dare to believe that He exists, only when they are experiencing difficult times, but once these situations are resolved they forget about Him again. Real faith comes from the heart through which we believe in Jesus as our Lord and Savior. If you were to conduct a survey around your neighborhood, asking people, "Do you believe in God?" Everyone will answer yes. Saying yes to this question doesn't assure them of their salvation because they are living in sin. The Word of God teaches that even demons believe in God and tremble before His presence; obviously, this knowledge and understanding that God exists doesn't save them. It is not enough to simply have a mental understanding about God's existence, but we have to believe in our heart, and confess with our mouth, that He is Lord, and then begin to live according to God's guidelines.

What do you have to do to receive salvation?

You must believe that Jesus is the only mediator between God and man. It is only through Him that you can receive the gift of salvation; He guarantees that you will go to heaven. You must confess Him with your mouth and receive Him in your heart.

What steps do you have to take to receive the gift of eternal salvation and to go to heaven?

a. You must repent of your sin.

"[13]He who covers his sins will not prosper, but whoever confesses and forsakes them will have mercy." *Proverbs 28.13*

b. You must confess your sin.

"[8]If we say that we have no sin, we deceive ourselves, and the truth is not in us. [9]If we confess our sins, He is faithful and just to forgive us our sins and to cleanse us from all unrighteousness." *1 John 1.8, 9*

c. You must confess Jesus as your Lord and Savior.

"[9]that if you confess with your mouth the Lord Jesus and believe in your heart that God has raised Him from the dead, you will be saved." Romans 10.9

If you have never invited Jesus into your heart, or if you are unsure of your salvation, and today you want to ask Jesus to come into your heart and receive the gift of eternal life, then repeat this prayer out loud:

"Heavenly Father, I recognize that I am a sinner and that my sin separates me from you. Right now, I confess with my mouth that Jesus Christ is Lord. I believe that God, the Father, raised Him from the dead. Jesus, I invite you to come into my heart and into my life. I break every covenant that I have made with the enemy, with my flesh and with the world. I repent of every sin I have committed, and right now, I receive the gift of salvation and eternal life." Amen.

2

What Happened When you Received Jesus as Your Lord?

Many believers, after inviting Jesus into their hearts, and repeating the sinner's prayer, begin to wonder what happened to them at that moment and what they should expect to happen next. I will now take the opportunity to guide you on your Christian walk, and as you grow and mature in God, you will bare much fruit for God's Kingdom. Everything you read in this book is in line with God's Word.

After inviting Jesus into your heart, many changes will begin to take place in your life. You might not always understand the changes, but I will explain what happened to you the moment that you made the decision to take this step of faith.

What happened when you received Jesus in your heart?

1. The new birth

The first thing that happened in your heart when you received Jesus as Lord and Savior was the new birth. This does not mean that you return to your mother's womb, it means that you were spiritually born again. God changes your "heart of stone" for a "heart of flesh" because He is the only one able to do such a thing.

The following verses confirm what you have just read:

"[3]Jesus answered and said to him, "Most assuredly, I say to you, unless one is born again, he cannot see the kingdom of God." [4]Nicodemus said to Him, "How can a man be born when he is old? Can he enter a second time into his mother's womb and be born?" [5]Jesus answered, "Most assuredly, I say to you, unless one is born of water and the Spirit, he cannot enter the kingdom of God. [6]That which is born of the flesh is flesh, and that which is born of the Spirit is spirit. [7]Do not marvel that I said to you, "You must be born again." John 3.3-7

"[25]Then I will sprinkle clean water on you, and you shall be clean; I will cleanse you from all your filthiness and from all your idols. [26]I will give you a new heart and put a new spirit within you; I will take the heart of stone out of your flesh and give you a heart of flesh. [27]I will put My Spirit within you and cause you to walk in My statutes, and you will keep My judgments and do them." Ezekiel 36.25-27

Humanity tries to change using human effort and strength, but without the help of the Holy Spirit, this change is impossible. God is the only one that is powerful enough to change your life and give you a new beginning, a new birth.

Jesus said, ***"You must be born again."*** Your choice of religion, membership in a church, the fact that you are a giver, or if you serve your priest or pastor, doesn't change the fact that you need to be born again to receive salvation in Christ.

You were spiritually born again the moment that you opened your heart to Jesus and invited Him in. "Does this mean that at that moment you became a perfect human being, or that you will never make a mistake or sin again? "The answer is NO". Only your spirit was born again at the moment you received Jesus in your heart; there are still many areas of your life, which you are going to have to deal with. You now have to continually want to grow in the knowledge of God, and for this to happen, you have to know what human beings are made of to be able to understand who you are. Later on in this book this subject will be covered in more detail.

2. You are God's children

After receiving Jesus as your Lord and Savior you are born again in God. You have been adopted as His child.

"[12]But as many as received Him, to them He gave the right to become children of God, to those who believe in His name: [13]who were born, not of blood, nor of the will of the flesh, nor of the will of man, but of God."
John 1.12, 13

Now, you are more than God's creation, you are His child, and as such, you have rights, privileges, authority and power in Him. You are now co-heir with Christ, and able to enjoy every blessing that was out of reach before your new birth because these blessings did not belong to you then. Now, every promise in God belongs to you, and this alone, is an incredible reason to rejoice. You are God's child!

3. **There is a hunger in you to know more about God**

The moment you received Jesus, as Lord of your life, an awakening in your heart took place, a hunger in your spirit to know more about God and His Word began to stir within you. Now you want to attend church and to tell everyone what you experienced. This is what happens when a person is born again. God places in your heart the desire to know Him intimately. This is a positive sign that you truly repented. Only a person who is genuine about his repentance of sin, and who opens his heart to Jesus, has the desire to know and understand the things of God.

4. You are a new creation

"[17]Therefore, if anyone is in Christ, he is a new creation; old things have passed away; behold, all things have become new." 2 Corinthians 5.17

When the Word of God teaches that you are a *new creation,* it is not saying that you will stop having bad thoughts or that you will never make another mistake or sin again. What these words mean is that now that you are a *new creature,* your heart has been renewed, or born again, but your soul still needs to be renewed daily.

Being a *new creature* means that the things you used to do, you will now choose not to do. The sin you used to practice before your new birth, you will now stop doing. If your sin was fornication, adultery, drunkenness, lies, stealing, jealousy, hate or blasphemy, to mention just a few, now you will not do these things again because you will feel repulsed to be involved in doing something that you know will hurt and offend your Lord. You will feel bad even thinking about doing such things. This is a sign that you are a new creature in Christ; you are born again.

5. You have a personal encounter with God

Millions of people know about God, they talk about Him, they say that they believe in their own way, but they have never experienced a personal encounter with the living God. As a result, God becomes one of many religions in which sin is practiced without guilt. To say that you believe in God in "your own way" is to have never experienced a personal encounter or relationship with God.

What does it mean to have a personal encounter with God? It means that you are now knowledgeable of the different facets of God, who He is as a friend, Father, brother, companion, Lord, healer, provider, and everything else that He is. You are now able to talk to Him directly without the need for an alternative intermediary. Jesus is the only mediator between God and man. You can feel His presence, which is now a very real experience in your life. You are now able to present your needs and anxieties before His throne of grace, in prayer, and know that He hears and answers your prayers. You know that He is with you wherever you are, and you feel His love. It is a wonderful thing to know Jesus personally. One thing that happens to you, and the reason you feel such joy, is precisely this personal relationship that you now enjoy with Him, the creator of heaven and earth. He is the only One who gives true joy and peace.

3

What Should You do Now That you are Saved?

Most people, after they are born again, are at a loss as to what to do next or what God expects of them. They have no idea what their responsibilities are now that they are God's children. In this chapter, you will learn a few basic principles that you should practice daily as you continue to grow in the Lord.

1. Study the Word of God

The Bible is God's personalized letter to you. It is the manual or guide that teaches you how to live your life. The Word of God is full of the right words that help you become a better parent, child, husband and wife. It teaches you how to have a personal relationship with God and how to live a prosperous and victorious life.

What are some questions you might have concerning the Bible?

a. What is the Bible?

The Bible is God's Word for your life.

"[12]For the word of God is living and powerful, and sharper than any two-edged sword, piercing even to the division of soul and spirit, and of joints and marrow, and is a discerner of the thoughts and intents of the heart." Hebrews 4.12

The Bible is also a group of books that were brought together and inspired by God.

"[15]...and that from childhood you have known the Holy Scriptures, which are able to make you wise for salvation through faith which is in Christ Jesus.
[16]All Scripture is given by inspiration of God, and is profitable for doctrine, for reproof, for correction, for instruction in righteousness."
2 Timothy 3.15, 16

The Bible is also a legal document used by God to establish His terms for the covenant that He made with His children. God teaches you, in His Word, what blessings He has prepared for you. Also, what your privileges, authority and promises are in Him. God tells you in His Word what benefits belong to you and to every believer.

b. Who wrote the Bible?

The Word of God was written by more than forty authors during a period of approximately

2000 years. Every author was inspired by God to write everything that He wanted us, His people, to know. Men made of flesh and bone wrote the Bible, but the inspiration for its contents came from God. Therefore, every word written in the Bible comes directly from God's heart; the Word is perfect from Genesis to Revelation.

"[20]knowing this first, that no prophecy of Scripture is of any private interpretation, [21]for prophecy never came by the will of man, but holy men of God spoke as they were moved by the Holy Spirit."
2 Peter 1.20, 21

c. How is the Bible divided?

The Bible is divided in two parts: The Old Testament or Old Covenant and the New Testament or New Covenant.

The word *testament* means pact.

d. How many books are in the Bible?

The Bible has **66 books,** which are divided by chapters and verses. The reason each book was divided this way was to make it easier for us to study it.

What is the purpose of the Word of God for the believer?

a. The Word teaches how to know, and understand, God's will for your life.

"[16]All Scripture is given by inspiration of God, and is profitable for doctrine, for reproof, for correction, for instruction in righteousness, [17]that the man of God may be complete, thoroughly equipped for every good work." 2 Timothy 3.16, 17

The Word of God gives the spiritual sustenance to every believer. This is easy to see throughout the Bible. God uses different elements or symbolism in His Word and calls it spiritual nourishment. The Word of God is a well-balanced diet. Let us take a look at a few examples of symbolism used in the Bible:

Milk	(1 Peter 2.2)
Honey	(Psalms 119.103)
Bread	(Luke 4.4)
Water	(Ephesians 5.26)
Meat	(Hebrews 5.12-14)

b. Can the Bible be trusted? Yes!

"[16]All Scripture is given by inspiration of God, and is profitable for doctrine, for reproof, for correction, for instruction in righteousness." 2 Timothy 3.16

"[5]Every word of God is pure; He is a shield to those who put their trust in Him. [6]Do not add to His words, lest He rebuke you, and you be found a liar." Proverbs 30.5, 6

Jesus said that His Word is trustworthy and dependable. You can fully rely on it because God stands by His Word.

"[35]Heaven and earth will pass away, but My words will by no means pass away." Matthew 24.35

God's spoken Word created the universe.

"[3]By faith we understand that the worlds were framed by the word of God, so that the things which are seen were not made of things which are visible." Hebrews 11.3

c. How should I study and learn from the Bible?

The Holy Spirit guides your life. He will show you how to study and learn from His Word, but allow me to give you a few practical pointers that will greatly help you in your journey:

- Begin by reading the New Testament, specifically with the gospels of Matthew, Mark, Luke and John.

- Meditate on the Word that you read and apply it to your life.

- When you read a verse or passage that impacts your life or that affects you deeply, meditate on it and confess the words daily.

- When you confess the Word, it becomes real in your life and it will bare forth fruit.

- Apply what you learn. It is worthless to read and memorize the Word if you don't live by it. If you don't practice what you read, then the Word will become simple head knowledge. God's Word will change your life if you practice and live what you read and hear.

"[24]Therefore, whoever hears these sayings of Mine, and does them, I will liken him to a wise man who built his house on the rock: [25]and the rain descended, the floods came, and the winds blew and beat on that house; and it did not fall, for it was founded on the rock. [26]"But everyone who hears these sayings of Mine, and does not do them, will be like a foolish man who built his house on the sand: [27]and the rain descended, the floods came, and the winds blew and beat on that house; and it fell. And great was its fall." Matthew 7.24-27

- Listen to taped messages. Your faith will increase and strengthen as you continually hear His Word.

  "Faith comes by hearing and hearing by the Word of God." Romans 10.17

  You might find yourself reading a verse or passage that is hard to understand, but as you grow in the Lord, your understanding will also increase. Ask the Holy Spirit to help you to understand His Word.

2. Begin to have a prayer life

There are several spiritual exercises that every new believer needs to practice and one of them is to pray every day. Your body needs daily exercise and nourishment to survive, grow and stay healthy. In this same way, believers also need their daily spiritual exercise to continue to grow healthy and strong in God.

What is prayer?
Prayer is a dialogue, a conversation with your Heavenly Father. Through prayer, you share with Him everything that is in your heart.

"[5]And when you pray, you shall not be like the hypocrites. For they love to pray standing in the

synagogues and on the corners of the streets, that they may be seen by men. Assuredly, I say to you, they have their reward. [6]But you, when you pray, go into your room, and when you have shut your door, pray to your Father who is in the secret place; and your Father who sees in secret will reward you openly." Matthew 6.5, 6

What is the difference between prayer and repeating something over and over again?

Repetitious prayer is the repetitive chanting of words. **Prayer** is talking and having a conversation with God. Your relationship and conversation with God is the same as the relationship between a father and son, and vice-versa. When you talk to God, there is no need to repeat mindless phrases over and over again. You can talk to Him the same way that a son speaks with his father, with freedom, expressing everything that is in your heart.

What steps should you take to pray effectively?

a. Pray to the Father in the name of Jesus.

"[23]And in that day you will ask Me nothing. Most assuredly, I say to you, whatever you ask the Father in My name He will give you." John 16.23

Every prayer must be directed to God in the name of Jesus. Otherwise, God can't hear you.

Why should you pray in the name of Jesus?

Jesus is the only man without sin, and although He is God in the form of a man, He died for your sin and was raised from the dead. His name is the only one that is recognized by God in heaven. If you ask God anything, in anybody else's name, God will not answer your prayer; He can't even hear it.

"12Nor is there salvation in any other, for there is no other name under heaven given among men by which we must be saved." Acts 4.12

Why the name of Jesus? What is so important about this name?

The name of Jesus has power and authority in heaven, on earth and beneath the earth:

- It has the power to heal

  "15And He said to them, "Go into all the world and preach the gospel to every creature. 16He who believes and is baptized will be saved; but he who does not believe will be condemned." Mark 16.15, 16

- It has the power to save
- It has the power to deliver the captives free
- It has the power to protect

- It empowers you to do anything He asks of you

b. Pray in line with the Word of God.

"[14]Now this is the confidence that we have in Him, that if we ask anything according to His will, He hears us. [15]And if we know that He hears us, whatever we ask, we know that we have the petitions that we have asked of Him."
1 John 5.14, 15

You can trust that when you ask anything of God, according to His will, He hears you. For instance, you know that it is God's will for you to be healed, delivered and prosperous. Therefore, if you ask God for healing, He will heal you. If you ask God for deliverance or for financial prosperity, He will do this too. You can be totally assured that when you ask God for anything that is in line with His Word, your prayer will be answered.

c. Pray with confidence and faith.

"[16]Let us therefore come boldly to the throne of grace, that we may obtain mercy and find grace to help in time of need." Hebrews 4.16

"[6]But without faith it is impossible to please Him, for he who comes to God must believe that He is,

and that He is a rewarder of those who diligently seek Him." Hebrews 11.6

God is your Heavenly Father. When you pray, don't approach Him with fear of being rejected or punished. Rather, approach Him with confidence and faith because He will hear you and give you the desires of your heart. He is your Father and He will give you what you are in need of.

d. Be thankful when you pray.

"[6]Be anxious for nothing, but in everything by prayer and supplication, with thanksgiving, let your requests be made known to God."
Philippians 4.6

When you finish asking God for the things that you need, you should end your prayer with thanksgiving because you know that He heard and answered your prayer. Every time you pray, remember to **give thanks to God** for listening to you and for His answer to your prayer.

e. Why should you pray?

- Prayer is important. You need it to develop your close and intimate relationship with God. You need to talk to God daily. This is how your relationship with your Heavenly Father will grow and strengthen.

- To ask God for the things that you need and to open the door to receive His blessings.

- To prevent falling into temptation.

"39Going a little farther, he fell with his face to the ground and prayed, "My Father, if it is possible, may this cup be taken from me. Yet not as I will, but as you will. 40Then he returned to his disciples and found them sleeping. "Could you men not keep watch with me for one hour?" he asked Peter. 41"Watch and pray so that you will not fall into temptation. The spirit is willing, but the body is weak."
Matthew 26.39-41

- To fight against the enemy.

What obstacles prevent God from hearing your prayers?

a. Unforgiveness

"25And whenever you stand praying, if you have anything against anyone, forgive him, that your Father in heaven may also forgive you your trespasses. 26But if you do not forgive, neither

will your Father in heaven forgive your trespasses." Mark 11.25, 26

If you have anything against someone else, God will not hear your prayers. You must **forgive** everyone that has offended you before God can forgive you.

What is forgiveness?

Forgiveness means to let go of a person who has offended you. It also means to loosen the person who caused you so much pain and to cancel a pending debt. Forgiveness is an act of will.

A few important principles about forgiveness are:

- Forgiveness is not an alternative; it is a command imposed by God.
- Unforgiveness is the enemy's trap.
- Unforgiveness is the cause for many physical ailments such as: arthritis, insomnia, ulcers, cancer, etc.
- Unforgiveness is the biggest obstacle in your prayer life.

- God will not listen to anyone who is angry with his brother. Therefore, you must forgive everyone who has offended you right now!

What steps do you need to take to forgive?

- Make the decision to forgive.
- Make a list of the people who have hurt you throughout your life.
- Express your forgiveness verbally.
- Repent for harboring unforgiveness in your heart.
- Rebuke every spirit of resentment, hate, bitterness, anger and anything else that the Holy Spirit places in your heart to renounce.

b. Doubt

"[6]But let him ask in faith, with no doubting, for he who doubts is like a wave of the sea driven and tossed by the wind. [7]For let not that man suppose that he will receive anything from the Lord." James 1.6, 7

What does doubt mean?

When you doubt, your mind and heart is divided among two thoughts. A doubt causes bewilderment and confusion, and it makes you wonder which road to take or what decision to make.

There is no room in your heart or mind to wonder if God is listening to you or not, or if it's true that God answers the prayers of His people. You can't be saying, "I think God hears me." The person who doubts is a person who is easily swayed from believing one thing or the other.

When you approach God, even though you can't see Him with your physical eyes, He is attentive to your prayers. You can't wonder if He is by your side or not. Think about what the Word tells you, He rewards those who seek Him diligently. Don't doubt. Everytime you approach Him in prayer, He will honor the desires of your heart.

A major obstacle in your prayer life is doubt. Stop it! Begin to believe His Word and He will bless you.

c. Spousal abuse

"7 Husbands, likewise, dwell with them with understanding, giving honor to the wife, as to the weaker vessel, and as being heirs together of the

grace of life, that your prayers may not be hindered." 1 Peter 3.7

When a husband or wife abuses his or her spouse verbally, emotionally or physically, it becomes a great obstacle in their lives. God can't hear their prayers.

Why?

Spousal abuse is the same as abuse to self because husbands and wives are one flesh. As God's child, you will also be mistreating Jesus if you abuse your spouse. If you want every prayer to be heard by God, then begin to treat your spouse well, in word and action.

d. Lack of commitment

Another obstacle to your prayers is your lack of commitment. People have a hard time making the commitment to pray everyday because prayer is not a priority in their lives, for this reason they can't prosper in God. To be committed in prayer means to make the decision to pray wholeheartedly and for a long time. Don't look back. Every believer must make the decision to pray for long periods of time and to get closer to God.

e. Lack of discipline

Believers need to learn to discipline themselves in their prayer time. To achieve a long and constant prayer time with God, you must discipline your body. Lack of discipline is a major enemy of your prayer time. Make the decision to pray at least fifteen to twenty minutes per day. Once you are comfortable with this amount of time, increase your prayer time until you achieve discipline in your prayer life and with God.

f. Lack of perseverance

"[18]praying always with all prayer and supplication in the Spirit, being watchful to this end with all perseverance and supplication for all the saints." Ephesians 6.18

"[1] Then He spoke a parable to them, that men always ought to pray and not lose heart." Luke 18.1

Lack of perseverance is a great enemy of the believer's freedom. Perseverance is an important virtue to develop in order to achieve success and an effective prayer life. Many people desire in their hearts to pray and they do it for two weeks, but after a while, they stop. This causes people to weaken in their spiritual walk and to fall into temptation.

Develop perseverance in life. Finish everything that you start and you will be a successful person. Regardless of how many obstacles the enemy tries to impose to stop your prayer life, don't give up and remain disciplined. Purpose in your heart to pray and to persevere until the end. Don't dismay. If you begin to notice that your prayers seem to go unanswered, then begin to believe God and His Word, then you will see surprising and wonderful results.

3. You need to attend your local church

"[25]...not forsaking the assembling of ourselves together, as is the manner of some, but exhorting one another, and so much the more as you see the Day approaching."
Hebrews 10.25

Many people don't give any importance to attending church because their beliefs are that God is everywhere, and while this is true because He is omnipresent, He doesn't manifest His glory or presence everywhere. Using this reasoning to stay away from church is wrong. Attending a spirit-filled church, where the Word of God is taught with boldness and clarity is very important.

What type of church should you attend?

You should visit, and become a part of, a Christian Evangelical church. It should be a church where the entire Word of God is believed and where His presence is manifested and felt. It should be a church that moves in the power of God, His joy and blessings.

What should be the essence of the church that you attend?

- The congregation must believe wholeheartedly that Jesus is the only way, truth and light and that no one comes to the Father except through Him.

  "[6]Jesus said to him, "I am the way, the truth, and the life. No one comes to the Father except through Me." John 14.6

- This church must believe and teach that Jesus came to this earth in the form of a man. He was crucified for our sins, was buried, and on the third day, God raised Him from the dead.

- This church must believe in the Holy Trinity. This consists in three people united for one purpose: the Father, the Son and the Holy Spirit.

"[19]Go therefore and make disciples of all the nations, baptizing them in the name of the Father and of the Son and of the Holy Spirit." Matthew 28.19

- It must believe in the baptism in water by immersion. Every believer needs to be baptized in water.

"[4]Therefore we were buried with Him through baptism into death, that just as Christ was raised from the dead by the glory of the Father, even so we also should walk in newness of life." Romans 6.4

- It must believe in the baptism of the Holy Spirit. After you are born again, there is a new experience waiting for you and this is to be filled by the Holy Spirit with the evidence of speaking in other tongues.

[8]But you shall receive power when the Holy Spirit has come upon you; and you shall be witnesses to Me in Jerusalem, and in all Judea and Samaria, and to the end of the earth." Acts 1.8

- The church that you attend must believe in divine healing as a sign of God's power.

"[15]And He said to them, "Go into all the world and preach the gospel to every creature." Mark 16.15

- It must believe that deliverance is the child's bread. God's will doesn't stop at salvation or healing, it also delivers you from the enemy's oppression.

- It must believe in the Second Coming of Christ, as the King of kings and Lord of lords.

- It must believe that the Bible is inspired by God, that it never changes and that it is the only authority of God for your life.

- The church must believe in the existence of heaven and hell.

  "[24]Then he cried and said, 'Father Abraham, have mercy on me, and send Lazarus that he may dip the tip of his finger in water and cool my tongue; for I am tormented in this flame.'" Luke 16.24

Why should you attend church?

a. **To be strengthened in God.** The best place to find strength and encouragement during the difficult times in your life is at church.

b. **To receive spiritual covering.** This means that you will have a pastor and a church that is praying for your protection, security and for you to receive the fullness of His blessings.

c. **To enjoy fellowship and friendship with brothers and sisters in the faith.** Now that you have received Jesus as your Lord and Savior, God gives you a new family, but to enjoy the benefits of this blessing, you must attend a church and introduce yourself to your new family and enjoy the fellowship and friendship with your new brothers and sisters.

"[1] Behold, how good and how pleasant it is for brethren to dwell together in unity! [2]It is like the precious oil upon the head, running down on the beard, the beard of Aaron, running down on the edge of his garments. [3]It is like the dew of Hermon, descending upon the mountains of Zion; for there the LORD commanded the blessing-- Life forevermore." Psalms 133.1-3.

d. **To praise and worship God.** You can praise God everywhere, but God designed a specific place called the church, where His children can gather together in harmony to adore and worship Him. The result of this joint worship in harmony is the outpouring of His blessings.

Church is not just a building where people meet. Church is the people you fellowship with. God gave each pastor and believer a church where they can come together to praise and worship Him.

"[1]Behold, how good and how pleasant it is for brethren to dwell together in unity! Psalms 133.1

e. **To study the Word of God.** The main reason why you should attend a church is to learn, study and grow in the knowledge of His Word. The Bible is the authority in your life and it will help you to grow spiritually. God has instituted apostles, prophets, teachers, pastors and evangelists to teach and instruct you in His Word.

4

What is God Expecting From You?

After receiving Jesus as Lord and Savior, the question that is asked most often is **"What is God expecting from me?"** The answer is simple. Jesus died on the cross to save you for a divine purpose. He did not lay down His life for you to sit in a church pew and keep it warm or to have you waste your time on temporary things.

What does He expect from you?

- **To evangelize**

  God expects you to share your testimony, what God has done in your life, with the people around you. There are people around you that feel the way you used to feel; they are empty, sad and in need of deliverance. They need what you have in Christ, a personal relationship with Jesus. God has chosen you as His precious instrument to evangelize.

Why should you share the Gospel with others?

Because God commands every believer to go out into the world and share the message of salvation to the lost.

"[15]And He said to them, "Go into all the world and preach the gospel to every creature. [16]He who believes and is baptized will be saved; but he who does not believe will be condemned." Mark 16.15, 16

This is the great commission, to evangelize everywhere you go and to every person you meet. Everybody has the right to know Jesus. You need to fulfill this great call on your life at home, at work, at church and around the world.

What backs you up when you share the Gospel with other people?

- The power of the Holy Spirit.

  "[8]But you shall receive power when the Holy Spirit has come upon you; and you shall be witnesses to Me in Jerusalem, and in all Judea and Samaria, and to the end of the earth." Acts 1.8

The Holy Spirit will give you the words to use when you testify and speak to others about Jesus. Before sharing your testimony or presenting the Gospel to anyone, you need to pray and ask the Lord to give you the words and the wisdom to do it.

Who should evangelize or share the Gospel?

Every believer, after receiving Jesus as Lord, has the responsibility to share the gospel. The good news about Jesus, and God's Word, should be shared with the people who haven't heard it.

What should you say?

Many people are under the mistaken belief that because they don't know much Bible text that they can't share the Gospel with anybody, but you have a powerful weapon on your side, it is your testimony. This is the first thing that you should share with other people because it is the living evidence of what God has done in your life. You have a first hand experience with God and you should be sharing it.

How do you share your testimony?

- Briefly **describe your background** and where you come from. In other words, describe the condition you were in, and with whom you related, before meeting the Lord. You can say something similar to: "I used to feel alone and rejected." "I used to feel depressed" or "I felt unworthy." Share what your life used to be like before Christ came into your heart.

- **Describe your need to find God**. What situation or event caused you to want to know God? Unfortunately, most people only look for God when they find themselves in a crisis situation. However, you can turn their sad moments into on opportunity to share with them your story and what motivated you to find God. For instance, "I wanted to die," "there was an emptiness in my life that I was unable to overcome on my own," and so on.

- **Describe the changes** that have taken place in your life since the day that you accepted Jesus as your Lord and Savior. When you tell your story, try to be as specific and concise as possible. Tell them the kind of person that you used to be, how you used to behave or how you handled yourself during times of crisis, before Christ and after. You can say something like: "before I received Jesus in my heart I felt alone and rejected, but now I feel joy and peace deep in my heart because I finally understand that I am not alone and that He doesn't reject me." Or, "I used to curse and smoke, but now I am free from that."

- **Share what your life is like, now that you walk with God.** Describe your first days and months at home, at church, at your job and how you felt as you started to learn more about your Heavenly Father.

- **Explain that Jesus used to occupy the last place in your life, but that Jesus is now a priority for you; He is Lord of your life.** You can't do anything without Him. You love Him more than you love your family, your job or anything else in life.

This is how you can share your testimony with other people. Through your spoken testimony, the people around you will know who Jesus is, Lord and Savior, and that His message of salvation is powerful. Make the decision today to share your testimony with someone who is close to you. Begin to practice the great commission given to you: to preach and teach the Gospel to every creature.

Knowing and talking about God has a **price**. You will be criticized and rejected by the people around you, including your family. Jesus was criticized and accused of being crazy. He said that you and I would also suffer the same persecution. You must be willing to pay the price of criticism and rejection.

"37He who loves father or mother more than Me is not worthy of Me. And he who loves son or daughter more than Me is not worthy of Me. 38And he who does not take his cross and follow after Me is not worthy of Me. 39He who finds his life will lose it, and he who loses his life for My sake will find it." Matthew 10.37-39

"37Jesus said to him, 'You shall love the LORD your God with all your heart, with all your soul, and with all your mind.'" Matthew 22.37

Who should you share your testimony with?

- With your family
- With your co-workers
- With your neighbors
- With your friends

5

Three Truths God Wants You to Know

There are very important truths that you should be aware of, now that you are a born again Christian. These truths are essential for your Christian life and maturity; they will strengthen you in God.

1. **Who you are in Christ**

    - You are God's child. John 1.12
    - You are justified. *Romans 5.1*
    - You are free. *Colossians 1.13*
    - God accepts you. *Ephesians 1.6*
    - You are the righteousness of God. *Ephesians 1.4*
    - God loves you. *John 3.16*
    - You are more than a conqueror. *Romans 8.37*
    - You belong to God's family. *Ephesians 2.19*
    - You are a new creature. *2 Corinthians 5.17*
    - You are saved and on your way to heaven. *Ephesians 2.8*
    - You are prosperous. *3 John 1.2*
    - You are healed. *Isaiah 53.3-5*

2. **You can do all things through Christ who strengthens you.** There is nothing impossible for you because He has promised to be with you. He

tells you in His Word that that you can do all things in Him.

"[13]I can do all things through Christ who strengthens me." Philippians 4.13

What can you do in Christ?

- You can change.

  "[6]...being confident of this very thing, that He who has begun a good work in you will complete it until the day of Jesus Christ." Philippians 1.6

- You can overcome every obstacle in your life.
- You can be free.
- You can fulfill your calling and purpose of God for your life.
- You can overcome every crisis and tribulation.
- You can do everything that God wants you to do.

  "[35]Who shall separate us from the love of Christ? Shall tribulation, or distress, or persecution, or famine, or nakedness, or peril, or sword? [36]As it is written: "For Your sake we are killed all day long; we are accounted as sheep for the slaughter."[37]Yet in all these things we are more than conquerors through Him who loved us." Romans 8.35-37

3. What you have in Christ

- You have eternal life. *1 john 5.13*
- You have power. *Acts 1.8*
- You have authority. *Luke 10.17-19*
- You have the armor of the Spirit. *Ephesians 6.10, 11*
- You have spiritual weapons. *2 Corinthians 10.4.* These weapons include the name of Jesus, the blood of Jesus, the power of the Holy Spirit, the Word of God and faith.
- You have the ability to live in righteousness. *1 Peter 2.24*
- You have God's protection. *Psalms 27.1*

6

What are Your Responsibilities as a New Believer?

You have learned what your privileges, blessings and rights are as a child of God. You now understand who you are, what you have, and what you can accomplish through Christ. In this chapter, you will learn what your responsibilities are as a child of God.

With every blessing that God showers upon you, He gives you new responsibilities, and for this to be in balance with His Word, you need to know what your blessings are in order to understand what your responsibilities are.

1. **Support your local church**

   The day that you received Jesus as your Lord and Savior, God placed you in a church with a pastor. You should support your new family in Christ with your resources, services, talents, abilities and prayer. The day you were born again, God also empowered you with gifts for you to use and bless your church.

2. **Tithes and offerings**

   Every time you hear someone teach on tithes and offerings, you will notice that most people become uncomfortable and defensive about it. However, tithes and offerings are the only basic, Biblical principles established by God to prosper you financially. God doesn't prosper you through bingo, the lottery or any other type of gambling activity.

What are tithes? Tithes are 10% of all your income.

What is an offering? An offering is the extra amount of money that you give after giving your tithes.

Where is this found in the Bible?

"8Will a man rob God? Yet you have robbed Me! But you say, "In what way have we robbed You?' In tithes and offerings. 9You are cursed with a curse, for you have robbed Me, even this whole nation. 10Bring all the tithes into the storehouse, that there may be food in My house, and try Me now in this," says the LORD of hosts, "If I will not open for you the windows of heaven and pour out for you such blessing that there will not be room enough to receive it." Malachi 3.8-10

You give your tithes and offerings of your own free will. Your salvation doesn't depend on you giving your tithes and offerings. However, when you choose not to obey His Word, and hold back

on your giving, you miss out on God's blessings for your life. Salvation is free for everyone who believes and receives Jesus as Lord, but to make sure that people hear the message of salvation is very costly. Radio and television airtime is very costly, as well as other means used by the church to spread the good news of Jesus Christ.

3. **Serve in church**

God has blessed you with a gift, talent or ability that you can use to serve your brothers and sisters in Christ. God expects you to use your own initiative to serve in any department or ministry in your church. **Why should you serve God? Because you are thankful to Him for all that He has done.**

"28Therefore, since we are receiving a kingdom which cannot be shaken, let us have grace, by which we may serve God acceptably with reverence and godly fear." Hebrews 12.28

Gratitude to the Lord for everything that He has done for you should inspire you to serve Him. You can't serve God by force; you serve Him because you are grateful. Get involved in your church and begin to serve today. Learn which ministries or departments are available in your church for you to begin serving today. If you have passion for music, children, the homeless, or any of the many ministries available, then join one and begin to bless others with your gifts and talents; this is the best way to offer your talents to God.

7

Questions That New Believers Ask Most Often

1. **What happens if I sin again?**

If you truly repent, wholeheartedly, then He forgives your sin. You have a lawyer who stands by your side, and intercedes on your behalf, in heaven, before your Heavenly Father, His name is Jesus.

"[9]If we confess our sins, He is faithful and just to forgive us our sins and to cleanse us from all unrighteousness. [10]If we say that we have not sinned, we make Him a liar, and His word is not in us." 1 John 1.9, 10

"[1]My little children, these things I write to you, so that you may not sin. And if anyone sins, we have an Advocate with the Father, Jesus Christ the righteous." 1 John 2.1

The fact that you are now a Christian doesn't mean that you are perfect; you will fail the Lord again. But, do not dismay, God provided the way for you to be cleansed once again, and it is through the blood of His Son, Jesus. The only pre-requisite that you need to do before God can forgive you of your sin is to truly repent of what you have done.

2. **Should I be baptized in water even though I was baptized as a child?**

The Word of God teaches that children should not be baptized in water because they are too young to understand what is happening. Children do not have the proper understanding of what is right or wrong. Jesus was presented in the temple when He was a child, but He was not baptized until He became an adult at the age of thirty. Children should be presented and dedicated to the Lord, but they should never be baptized.

"[22] Now when the days of her purification according to the law of Moses were completed, they brought Him to Jerusalem to present Him to the Lord." Luke 2.22

This verse confirms that Jesus was brought into the temple and presented to God by His parents.

"[21]When all the people were baptized, it came to pass that Jesus also was baptized; and while He prayed, the heaven was opened. [22]And the Holy Spirit descended in bodily form like a dove upon Him, and a voice came from heaven which said, "You are My beloved Son; in You I am well pleased." Luke 3.21, 22

Before you can be baptized in water, you must have knowledge and understanding of what you are about to do. Children lack the understanding of what is right or wrong, and because of this reason, they should not be baptized in water.

a. **Should Christians be baptized?** Yes.

Why should Christians be baptized?

- Because God commanded it.

  "[19]Go therefore and make disciples of all the nations, baptizing them in the name of the Father and of the Son and of the Holy Spirit." Matthew 28.19

- Baptism is a sign that demonstrates your desire to have a clean and renewed conscience.

- Because Jesus was baptized.

  "[13]Then Jesus came from Galilee to John at the Jordan to be baptized by him." Matthew 3.13

- Baptism is an external confession of what has happened in your past, a demonstration of your willingness and desire to break from it, and a declaration that you will never look back.

"[16]He who believes and is baptized will be saved; but he who does not believe will be condemned." Mark 16.16

b. When should you be baptized?

You should be baptized immediately after receiving Jesus as Lord.

"[36]Now as they went down the road, they came to some water. And the eunuch said, "See, here is water. What hinders me from being baptized?" [37]Then Philip said, "If you believe with all your heart, you may." And he answered and said, "I believe that Jesus Christ is the Son of God." [38]So he commanded the chariot to stand still. And both Philip and the eunuch went down into the water, and he baptized him." Acts 8.36-38

c. Where should you be baptized?

You should be baptized in a place where you can be totally submerged in water.

d. In whose name should you be baptized?

In the name of the Father, the Son and the Holy Spirit.

"[19]Go therefore and make disciples of all the nations, baptizing them in the name of the Father and of the Son and of the Holy Spirit." Matthew 28.19

3. **What happens if there is an area of your life in which you don't feel free?**

You need inner healing and deliverance. (Man is a three-part being: **spirit, soul and body**).

Why do you need inner healing and deliverance? Because the day that you were born again only your spirit was saved, but your soul still needs to be transformed.

"[23] Now may the God of peace Himself sanctify you completely; and may your whole spirit, soul, and body be preserved blameless at the coming of our Lord Jesus Christ." 1 Thessalonians 5.23

What is the spirit?

The spirit is the inner man, the part of you that was made a new creature in Him, and through which you communicate with God, the Father, and where the Holy Spirit now resides.

"[27]The spirit of a man is the lamp of the LORD, searching all the inner depths of his heart." Proverbs 20.27

What is the soul?

The soul is your will, emotions and mind. This is the part of you that was not born again; it needs to be renewed and transformed.

"[21]Therefore, lay aside all filthiness and overflow of wickedness, and receive with meekness the implanted word, which is able to save your souls." *James 1.21*

What should you do with your soul?

- **Renew it** through God's Word.

- **Transform it.** *"[1]I beseech you therefore, brethren, by the mercies of God, that you present your bodies a living sacrifice, holy, acceptable to God, which is your reasonable service. [2]And do not be conformed to this world, but be transformed by the renewing of your mind, that you may prove what is that good and acceptable and perfect will of God. [3]For I say, through the grace given to me, to everyone who is among you, not to think of himself more highly than he ought to think, but to think soberly, as God has dealt to each one a measure of faith."*
  Romans 12.1-3

Your mind needs to be renewed and your soul needs inner healing and deliverance. Your emotions might be hurting as a consequence of traumatic experiences from your past that might include physical, sexual or emotional abuse, incest, etc. Your emotions also need to be renewed.

Many of you might be dealing with rejection, unforgiveness, bitterness or hate; you need help in healing your soul from the pain of your past. My advice to you is that you seek help. If you are suffering from emotional problems, or perhaps you are addicted to pornography, drugs or any other problem or generational curse, then you need to remember that you are not alone, you can overcome all of these things in the name of Jesus and with His power.

4. **Is there any other experience after receiving Jesus and being baptized in water?**

Yes, the experience of **the baptism in the Holy Spirit** awaits you, with the evidence of speaking in tongues.

Why is the baptism of the Holy Spirit necessary?

- To be empowered from above.

"[1]When the Day of Pentecost had fully come, they were all with one accord in one place. [2]And suddenly there came a sound from heaven, as of a rushing

mighty wind, and it filled the whole house where they were sitting. [3]Then there appeared to them divided tongues, as of fire, and one sat upon each of them. [4]And they were all filled with the Holy Spirit and began to speak with other tongues, as the Spirit gave them utterance." Acts 2.1-4

How do you receive the baptism of the Holy Spirit?

- **By faith.** You will receive the baptism of the Holy Spirit in the same way that you received the gift of salvation, by faith. The evidence that you received this gift is that you will begin to speak in other tongues.

Who receives the baptism of the Holy Spirit?

- **Every one who believes, can receive the Holy Spirit.**

"[17]And these signs will follow those who believe: In My name they will cast out demons; they will speak with new tongues." Mark 16.17

Receive it by faith right now!

What is the purpose for receiving the baptism of the Holy Spirit?

- To receive the power to testify.

"[8]...But you shall receive power when the Holy Spirit has come upon you; and you shall be witnesses to Me in Jerusalem, and in all Judea and Samaria, and to the end of the earth." Acts 1.8

- The baptism of the Holy Spirit transforms, sanctifies, and cleanses.

- It makes Jesus and His Word come alive.

- It improves your prayer life.

"[26]Likewise the Spirit also helps in our weaknesses. For we do not know what we should pray for as we ought, but the Spirit Himself makes intercession for us with groanings which cannot be uttered. [27]Now He who searches the hearts knows what the mind of the Spirit is, because He makes intercession for the saints according to the will of God."
Romans 8.26, 27

Conclusion

The Christian life involves the constant pursuit of establishing a closer and more intimate relationship with Jesus Christ our Lord; it is to live apart from sin and to choose to live righteous lives that please God. We need to learn to depend on Him completely and not to lose heart when we face difficulty in life because He is our reward for remaining steadfast.

Unfortunately, many people begin this marathon, but give up before crossing the finish line. Jesus said, *"He who perseveres until the end shall be saved."* Never allow the enemy to rob His Word from you; stand firm and use the authority and power given to you, by God, to fight; never give up because your reward is near. God tells us to have courage and to be strong. There will be many pitfalls in your daily walk with God, you might fail many times, or be rejected by the people around you, you might even be betrayed by someone close to you, but remember, He overcame the world, He will never leave you nor forsake you. Keep your eyes fixed on God and you will cross the finish line.

Perhaps this new path, that you now walk, might seem harsh at times. Perhaps some of the difficult circumstances in your life might seem hopeless, but remember that it is during the hardest times of your life that you should be closest to God. He is your strength and shelter during times of despair; there is victory in Him. He is the God of all impossibilities. Whatever the situation you might be going through, whether good or bad, happy or sad, He will turn it around and make it the instrument that He will use to help you grow and mature in Him.

"[13]… the unity of the faith and of the knowledge of the Son of God, to a perfect man, to the measure of the stature of the fullness of Christ." Ephesians 4.13

In the end you will be able to say:

"[7]I have fought the good fight, I have finished the race, I have kept the faith. [8]Finally, there is laid up for me the crown of righteousness, which the Lord, the righteous Judge, will give to me on that Day, and not to me only but also to all who have loved His appearing." 2 Timothy 4.7

The amplified Bible says,

"[7]I have fought the good (worthy, honorable, and noble) fight, I have finished the race, I have kept (firmly held) the faith. [8][As to what remains] henceforth there is laid up for me the [victor's] crown of righteousness [for being right with God and doing right], which the Lord, the righteous Judge, will award to me and recompense me on that [great]

day--and not to me only, but also to all those who have loved and yearned for and welcomed His appearing (His return). 2 Timothy 4.7

Bibliography

Biblia de Estudio Arco Iris. Version Reina-Valera, Revision 1960, Biblical Text copyright© 1960, Sociedades Bíblicas in Latin America, Nashville, Tennessee, ISBN: 1-55819-555-6.

Biblia Plenitud. 1994 Editorial Caribe, Nashville, TN 37214, ISBN: 9780899222813.

Diccionario Español a Inglés, Inglés a Español. Editorial Larousse S.A., Printed in Dinamarca, Núm. 81, México, ISBN: 2-03-420200-7, ISBN: 70-607-371-X, 1993.

El Pequeño Larousse Ilustrado. 2002 Spes Editorial, S.L. Barcelona; Editions Larousse, S.A. de C.V. México, D.F., ISBN: 970-22-0020-2.

Expanded Edition the Amplified Bible. Zondervan Bible Publishers. ISBN: 0-31095168-2, 1987 – Lockman Foundation USA.

Reina-Valera 1995 - Edición de Estudio, (United States of America Sociedades Bíblicas Unidas) 1998.

Strong James, LL.D, S.T.D., Concordancia Strong Exhaustiva de la Biblia, Editorial Caribe, Inc., Thomas Nelson, Inc., Publishers, Nashville, TN - Miami, FL, USA, 2002. ISBN: 0-89922-382-6.

The New American Standard Version. Zordervan Publishing Company, ISBN: 0310903335.

The Tormont Webster's Illustrated Encyclopedic Dictionary. ©1990 Tormont Publications.

Vine, W.E. *Diccionario Expositivo de las Palabras del Antiguo Testamento y Nuevo Testamento.* Editorial Caribe, Inc./División Thomas Nelson, Inc., Nashville, TN, ISBN: 0-89922-495-4, 1999.

Ward, Lock A. *Nuevo Diccionario de la Biblia.* Editorial Unilit: Miami, Florida, ISBN: 0-7899-0217-6, 1999.

OUR VISION

GMI PUBLICATIONS

The objective of our mission is to spiritually feed God's people through preaching and teaching and to take the Word of God everywhere it is needed.

LEADERS THAT CONQUER

Guillermo Maldonado
ISBN: 1-59272-023-4*

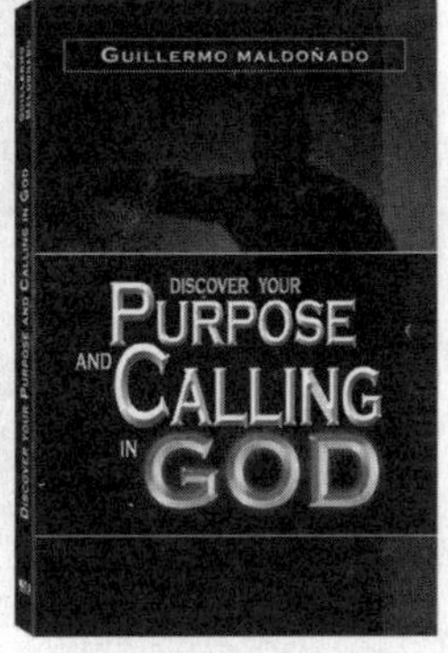

DISCOVER YOUR PURPOSE AND CALLING IN GOD

Guillermo Maldonado
ISBN: 1-59272-019-6

FORGIVENESS

Guillermo Maldonado
ISBN: 188392717-X*

THE FAMILY

Guillermo Maldonado
ISBN: 1-59272-024-2

SUPERMATURAL EVANGELISM

Guillermo Maldonado
ISBN: 159272013-7

BIBLICAL FOUNDATIONS FOR A NEW BELIEVER

Guillermo Maldonado
ISBN: 1-59272-005-6

** Books available also in Spanish and French.*